LIBRARY
NEW COLLEGE OF CALIFORNIA
777 VALENCIA STREET
SAN FRANCISCO, CA 94110
(415) 626-1694

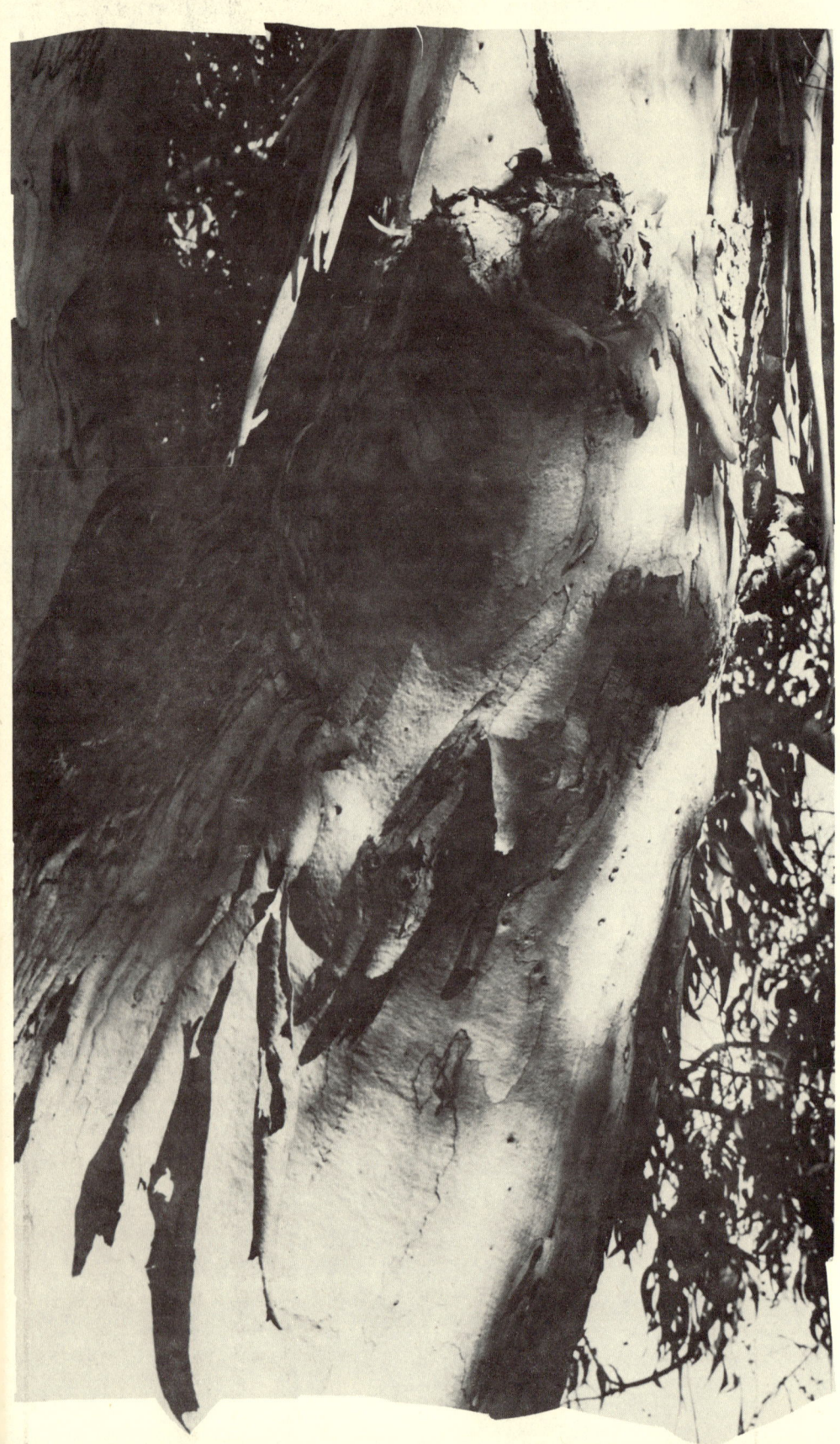

LANGUAGE OF A SMALL SPACE

Poetry
by
Deirdre Sharett

> "The poetic image places us at
> the origin of the speaking being."
>
> -- Gaston Bachelard
> THE POETICS OF SPACE

HARTMUS PRESS
MILL VALLEY, CALIF.
1980

© Hartmus Press
Printed in the USA
All rights revert to author

ISBN 0-915868-01-6

Acknowledgements:

Some of these poems have appeared (occasionally in earlier versions) in the following publications:
BEATITUDE, THE MARINER, THE OPEN READER, WOMEN TALKING/WOMEN LISTENING, SHEAF, CAYATI, and DEAR GENTLEPERSONS: A COLLECTION OF BAY AREA WOMEN POETS

Hartmus Press
23 Lomita Dr.
Mill Valley, Calif. 94941

for Fire / for Light
    and for my daughters
        who understand the mutiny now

CONTENTS

HOUSE WITH CRACKED WALLS

The Fish Speared Bleeds	1
It is the Floors	2
Now That the Truth is Out	3
Growing Sad at Midnights	4
Togetherness Voyage Interrupted	5
No—Fault Severing	6
This Raft Rides Low	7
Mutiny	8
The House with Cracked Walls	9

LOVERS AND OTHER LONELINESS

The Hermit	13
To a First—Rate Fisherman	14
Love, I've Been Sad	15
Strip (No) Tease	16
One if by Land	17
Marked	19
Visit to Vesuvios	20
Seeing You Tonight	21
Journeying to Oakland	22
The Task of Ashes	24
Do It Yourself	25
An Account of Who We Are	26
In This Dark Room	27
Sugar and Ash	29
After Our Fight	30
All Night the Icy Quarter Moon ...	31
I Hear You Finally	32
End of the Auction	33
This Carnage Repeats Itself	34
Such Men Are Dangerous	35
Cocks Crow	36

OUT OF ALL THIS

It is Out of All This	39
This Exclusive Monogamous One–To–One Relationship	40
Letter, Unsent	41
Within Us Things Grow	42
After You Leave, I Rise	43
The Skin of This Animal	44
Ticking	45
Lunar Delusion	46
Snake Trail in the Dusty Road	47
The Voyeur In Search of a Life	48
What Has Been Engineered	51
Words After a Lapse in Writing During Which I Move From One House to Another	52
Moved In At Last	53
Another Calamity	54
What Are You Doing Here	55
Decisions	56
They Were, He Was, She Was	57
Love Again	59
Language of a Small Space	60
Ode to Romantic Poetry	61
The Awe–Filled Wounds	62

I.

HOUSE WITH CRACKED WALLS

"once the last absolutes were torn to pieces
you could begin"

... Adrienne Rich
"November 1968"

THE FISH SPEARED BLEEDS

The fish speared
bleeds knowledge of swimming
and dies with no questions

The frog jumps
without guarantee
No light illuminates
his landing

With the tides
sea anemones open
and close

We are forever
    reflecting
    dissecting
    deciding

Consequences like tigers
spring
between our choices.

IT IS THE FLOORS,

the floors that keep dissolving,
keep falling
out from under;
yes   one foot down
and the next step is forever —
or into yesterday ...

It's not the whole house —
with the pans of roast beef
odoring the kitchen;
not the walls
that stand as solid
and upright as ever;
And the ceiling is adept
at keeping its
respectful distance.

But the floors:
wooden planks keep cracking up
like ice floes
the fancy carpet
folding
below the waves
until you don't know where
to stand   or how
knees locked
or bent
to spring and balance
with the rocking
underneath ...

It's all impossible.
Looking in
through the calmly parted
curtains,
who would know?

NOW THAT THE TRUTH IS OUT

Now that the truth is out
I could flay her
Stripping skin like bark
I want to watch
her twig body jerk
      Not picture the oily
      snake—sex undulations
      with you in her bed

I wonder if I would wither
her garden of fresh smiles
as I pull finger nails:
      You love her
      You love me not

All those phone calls
with their special signals
catching you on the sticky
threads she wove
the whispers of hemlock
in your ear:
      Life would be roses with her
      Life would be thorns with me

I could easily take
the top of her head off
and THAT would be poetry.

GROWING SAD AT MIDNIGHTS,

when the sky descends
to sit heavy on each stone
I breathe in the ice
of stars
A brujo has told me
it's the path with the heart
I should follow
I have taped his voice
for future consideration
and gather back my footsteps
filled with ashes

We face each other
museums with closed doors
the road always tenuous
now dropped away .
Paused before tomorrow
I think about hearts and paths
knitting my nights
with nostalgia
Such rotting wool
keeps out no wind

Midnight
    the top spinning
    the hovering bird
    the coin on its edge.

TOGETHERNESS VOYAGE INTERRUPTED

The explosion of choices
all the strewn parts
of decisions   that blast
the past into bits
the floating debris
consequences
coloring all these muddied waters
The oars have turned to putty
in their locks
and bend like water snakes
in swamp grass

We have not yet
recognized the course of fear
determined the fault of stars
accepted the price of beans

It is the Golden Age of Anger
with or without Greek choruses
There were the fatal flaws
hissing:
Stupidity says the father
Sloth says the mother
Separateness says the husband
Selfishness say the children
Labels that shred the mind
singe the skin

It is not laughter
that plays on the waves
like froth
It is the decaying rodent
tossing in the wake
of this harsh cruise.

NO-FAULT SEVERING

Corrosion
may deaden
the edge of
these cuts
and translation
will change
his/story.

But for now
the shivering skin
along the trim
division
still quivers
with nerves
barely kenning
this ending.

Along this fault
that no one
owns
the pieces
part.

THIS RAFT RIDES LOW

This raft rides low in the water.
People are scraped away from it.
Set adrift in the waves
they sink into salt.

Still
there is no quiet.

Under the sullen surface
wet mountains
crash shouting against the skin.
Memories swim   loudly persistent.
The peelings cling to the paint.

Nothing cuts clean.
Nothing cleanses.

MUTINY

I have traded the kitchen
for a classroom
cracking the shell at mid—life
to birth
a mutant self.

One of my daughters has gone
to live with her father.

Hostile house
the stove grows grease
the refrigerator gathers frost
dishes pile
grass lengthens
wires corrode
plumbing overflows.

Trying to juggle
house   people   self
I don't notice
how even my daughters
want me back
in my shell
It is made of bars
of chalk dust words
like   MOTHER
they accuse me
of erasing.

THE HOUSE WITH CRACKED WALLS

                -- from the painting by
                Paul Cézanne

What has escaped this place
flying out through the black
cracks in those walls
leaving the cold dark rooms
to give up their hold
        their ghosts
        their crumbling reasons

Outside
the hot stones glow
something reaches toward sky
The trees shake with it.

II.

LOVERS AND OTHER LONELINESS

"Our bones are lightning
in the night of the flesh.
O world, all is night,
life is the lightning."

... Octavio Paz
"Live Interval"

(translation Muriel Rukeyser)

THE HERMIT

Journeys always start
badly
I always worry
carry too much baggage
This time I take
only my staff
and lantern

When we meet
our lanterns
shimmer together
defying the darkness
of trees

I shiver under
the words spilling
out of your cowl:
   "The road behind you
    is closed"

Your lantern flickers
I shield it
from the night wind
wanting to wander
in tandem

I have hidden
below stones
surveyed the undersides
of moss
I am used to cool
dark places

It is time
to leave all that
My lantern flickers
I yield it
to the night wind
When the sun rises
I am alone.

TO A FIRST-RATE FISHERMAN

I who had sounded
and was barely turning up
from that spongy floor
saw from my sea cave
your lures
flashing metal bright in the sun waves
breaking through the surface of my ocean
moving through the sea light
beckoning   beckoning.

I heard the murmur of your words
curl round my edges
like a winding sheet.
It's clear not only Sirens
but Ulysses too could sing.

Wanting to twine with you
like seaweed   to be held
to feel the shark's teeth
of your smile
I bit.
It severed my connection with pain
for a smile's instant.

You fish well   I see now
you troll constantly
though I never noticed that before.
I flop awkwardly in air.
You don't know what to do
now that you've reeled me in.

Slowly   I unhook myself
and swim back out to sea
relearning   salt   water.

LOVE, I'VE BEEN SAD

too long
tonight I want
to smile
forget the well below
my laugh
from which
I crank
each morning's
icy water.

Hold me
skin close
bone to bone
while the world
blurs.

STRIP (NO) TEASE

When the clothes come off
I say — perhaps a bit flippant
you see before you a real
live woman
But I mean it
nothing plastic
I am real
as a blade of grass
my pain
shows in my eyes
and spills over
often.

If I were into taking
better care of myself
I might avoid
encounters
I would hole up
But I am going
back to school
I study
me.

I walk softly
on this planet
don't want to miss
any messages.

ONE IF BY LAND

Under my feet the sand pulls
away   the water swelling
against my ankles   slides
back out to sea   tugging at me
to join the sun
where yesterday was swallowed.
My eyes float with the moon
toes clinging to the sand
like roots
of some exotic plant.
(Think of the Venus Flytrap.)

This is no Normandy
but I plead guilty
to attempted invasion.
I have scrutinized your landscape
for cracks
in which to grow
like moss
tried to weave my webs
between your fingers
to hide under your tongue
and whisper   I love you's
back   at me.
(Remember how I played both parts.)

I wanted
to be indispensable
to your knees   wanted
you at attention
for me alone.
Oh I tried to indent you
impress you with me!

You are not moved
though loneliness is all
I want to conquer.
You drink your fear
down in jiggers.
My fingers release.
Dreams pop like balloons
on the edges of the box
you   are nailing shut
around your heart.

MARKED

I wake this morning
the covers shared
in unfamiliar tangles
my red—lined skin
a roadmap
from a dreamless night.

Not like the creases
in my palms,
these life—lines
traverse my arms
shoulders
breasts
crossing me
with temporary trails.

The mirror
in the bathroom
with its spidery
silver pattern
shows me other lines
more permanent —
though nothing is.

I pull this skin
imprinted by too many
wrinkled sheets
along.
Seek somewhere dark
to shed it.

VISIT TO VESUVIOS

At two it is time
to spill out of the wine glass
where i have been hiding
watching my reflection
in the eye of this hurricane

When i stand parts of me
slide to the floor
i gather all these scraps
into piles and begin to staple
fingers to hands
toes to feet   and so on
i paper clip my muscles
to my bones
finally pinning my skin on
overall
then walk into the street

Later — maybe when they
have dried — will be time
for glazing the marbles
of my eyes
sinking them back into the
shadowed footsteps in my face
They have washed out again
like two glass floats.

SEEING YOU TONIGHT,

my skin flinched inward
where you touched me;
your hand bent the bones
of all my resolutions.
Oh the charts are still available
the channels not closed off —

and I fear if you desired it
I would try once again
to flow into your veins
like honey
if you said the right things
I would swim once more
between your knees.

JOURNEYING TO OAKLAND

I am journeying to Oakland
under the hot June sun
to find the Women's Press Collective
This is the first time
I have driven
this frozen arch.

>Yesterday I read Judy Grahn:
>"A Woman Is Talking to Death".
>Is this the bridge
>the cyclist died on?

Oakland, it has taken
all these years for me
to get here
and I made it by collecting
all my pieces
putting them behind a car wheel
armed with school books
and a map.

>I am so scared
>of endings
>I am tempted
>never to begin...
>Never without pain
>the letting go.
>I saw an old lover
>the other day
>and I remembered.

Oakland you are hiding
a Women's Press Collective
in a sagging once—white
building I have come to
by outsmarting
one—way streets.
Up three flights of stairs

past the Chinese sewing company
behind a door I never found.

        It's easy to see where
        the plaids don't match.
        Why even pretend
        these joinings can occur
        without distortion?

Oakland, Gertrude Stein has wronged you;
you are definitely there.
Guarded by wire voices
alternating yes and no,
it's the Women's Press Collective
that is missing.

        Something there is
        that doesn't like
        a wall, Frost said
        and all these differences
        bristle between us.

        Is it not suspicious
        how much we want agreement
        this desire to be similar
        like finding the road

    home again.

THE TASK OF ASHES

After the stilled
flutterings
of a hundred random fires
we are given time
to gather
the bits of bone and grist
needed
to refill our rash baskets.

It is the task
of ashes
to render all things
renewable.

DO IT YOURSELF

We were, perhaps, as warm
as might be expected
bringing as we do
all those old movies
Oh yes, we each remember
how this one ends
The car, filled with ghosts,
grows colder
Silence between the windowpanes
grows shatterproof
You sit thick   unmappable
I spiral into myself
pulling my wandering thoughts after:
a trackless crawler
looking for water

The strange mist between us
congeals

I move slowly from the car
You move slowly from the car
I echo the nonchalance
of your voice
You reflect the noncommittal angle
of my words
I mirror the stillness
of your arms
You mimic the cool mechanics
of my legs

We do not break out of this dream,
receding from each other

The movie reels on
I walk into an empty house
thinking how   in the end
I am always left stroking
my own bones.

AN ACCOUNT OF WHO WE ARE

The vultures that hover
above all our moves
know nothing of love
They eat the living liver
out of Prometheus
bringer of fire

You and I make occasional magic
this instant suspended
fending off death
with feathery fingers
adhesive thighs

At two in the morning
I want you so much
I taste your skin like metal
in my mouth
You   so newly minted
fragile and magnetic
rejecting bottled nectars
you are tougher than me
with your unfiled inward—leaning
edges

I travel dreading
the final inevitable calming
the cold coagulation
of the blood
I fear lest the honeyed juices
thicken in their cells
wanting to spend them
I have no use for banks
as I watch my shadow lengthen
and the days fall.

IN THIS DARK ROOM

It's not only time   each day
crossed off

not only old love gone

but You and I
coupling
and uncoupling
in this dark room

> Sometimes I feel like a boxcar
> and the ride ahead is short
> These days
> Omaha
> is not so far away

The blankets on this bed
can smother fear
an hour
maybe two
but You and I
coupling
and uncoupling

> Yesterday
> I didn't even know you
> and today
> I fear another loss
> Tomorrow will be

        is

   was

 just / like / that

I fear the last uncoupling
and all the rusty hitches

lying about the corners
of dark barns
and You and I
coupling
and uncoupling
in this dark room
under these blankets
smothering fear.

SUGAR AND ASH

1.

Early morning light flickers through the thin
fringe of half parted apricot curtains,
licking the shadows away from your skin.

Your hair, curly and red, ignites
in the summer sun beginning to torch
this resistant room.
I reach over to touch you
tracing your body with privileged fingers.

Suddenly I realize
I have not canned fruit for the winter
hoarded sugar against the shortage.

2.

Brushing my cheek with the smell
of pine soap and tobacco, your tanned arm
stretches to my side of this hungry bed.
I feel the stirring, the awesome so wonderful
stirring.

Our bodies swim toward each other
treading the miraculous waters
one last time   until
clock and calendar fully thrust upon us
this fiery day: it's ashen divergence
of paths.

AFTER OUR FIGHT

Four days ago you brought a yellow rosebud
clutched in your teeth like Carmen as you rode
the metal wind up the hill to my house.
Now the petals curl back to reveal the blossom's center;
it is withering.
Perhaps nothing can survive so much exposure.

I saw the moon rise orange, full tonight.
Tomorrow it will start to wane.
We were to watch it from the courtyard, but you've gone.
The clock ticks midnight.
It is an earth of dying we are born to.

This morning I gathered blackberries alone for breakfast
and felt ahead to some strange life I hesitate to live.
Responsible to no one; my own calendar.
No one to disappoint. No fear of loss.

This afternoon I noticed peanut butter
and your crackers sitting on the shelf.
And near my bed tonight, your book
due Friday at the library.
Shall I call you? Or take it back myself?

I was just wondering   as I sat here
at the glass table
sipping my tea
alone.

```
        all
      night
       the
     icy
     quarter
     moon
      an
        empty
            boat


                my skin
              is lonely
              i want
                to reach out
                        and touch
                your face
                    again
                need
                    to thaw
                        this frozen
                            body
                    i feel like
                crawling
              into your bed
            no matter
            who's there
                i'll just
                    settle
                        in the
                                cracks
                    between you
                and warm
                myself
              in your
                    heat.
```

I HEAR YOU, FINALLY

I am tired of examinations
contrasting passion
with proper decisions
the ones my veins never
agree with.
Humor coating sadness
like ointment
only keeps the air from getting in.
My anger is loud. My pain untidy.
You are right; I am not
civilized.

Labelling my words
a grade B movie
you have rendered judgement
from the tip of your upended nose.
No matter that your feet flap
loosely in your sandals.
You are polished indeed.
The hair flowing freely
to your shoulders only
hides the tightness
of your high brow.

Speak to me in Latin.
Quote to me from Pound.

END OF THE AUCTION

It is the last month
of this cutting year
The minutes shrink past
that quilted time
of infinite nights
Behind your left shoulder
and mine   the spectre
is already visible

This threadless season
calendars no days

It is a time of no commitment
Men like rabbit puppets
shadowing my walls
fearful of intimacy
and too much attachment

What remains is spare
and occasional
as your body
met perhaps weekly
perhaps not

The years ahead loom lean
and sparsely furnished
a bankrupt bohemian's
decaying mansion
the best pieces
already sold off.

THIS CARNAGE REPEATS ITSELF

You fire low
across my bow
a warning
to whatever
crawls forward
to be cured

Afloat the fishes
of desire
move the rocks
dead they stink
like three—day
guests

The gnats of all
my sunken boats
echo their
moldy buzz.

SUCH MEN ARE DANGEROUS

Men with thirsty smiles
that lean and hungry look
lurking
in artful eyes
swirl out of shadows
spinning
the plausible lie

Sometimes it's omission
commas
left out
avoidance
of the significant
detail
They steer my assumptions
with craft

And then there are those
who speak the truth
only momentary of course
and nothing
to depend on.

COCKS CROW

after D.H.Lawrence

Cocks crow
and split the middle of the world
asunder with their cry
turn black to dawn
And I am drawn by some dark fever
to bid them enter
And I do then   as any hen
to hear that cry
gurgle within my loins.

I like to feel the sunrise
the dawn's hot rays explode the baffled darkness
I want my own bars lifted
as the cry is hammered home
pounding at purple doors
bone calming bone.

Night spent at last
lightless this gray–black rising
We break no other fast, share no nutritious bread
The music that I thought we both
could hear
was sounding just for me
False trumpets
And the cocks crow   fear.

III.

OUT OF ALL THIS

"In a dark time, the eye begins to see."

... Theodore Roethke

"We must talk now. Fear
Is fear. But we abandon one another."

... George Oppen
"Leviathan"

IT IS OUT OF ALL THIS

It is out of all this
i want to make sense

Looking for truth

Slender trails of slime
i follow
        drying spoor
                before
i reach any goal
        goaded by black wings
                and the ticking

The gadget fidget
                got me
                      so many years

Try to forget reason
trade it for skin
                and risky visions

But there is the buzz

What circle of columns
                pillows my tomorrows
bars i can bang
                my bones against.

THIS EXCLUSIVE MONOGAMOUS ONE-TO-ONE RELATIONSHIP

Somehow I always think it's reducible:
an apple to be nibbled away at
with questions and answers
Or compactible:
a down jacket to be jammed
into a stuff bag
Or maybe it is bridgeable:
by agreements   compromises
constructs come to
through deliberation and decision.
How to lessen distance between us.

What is unknown melts:
an icecube in hot tea.
For instance:
you lying between my legs.
What needs knowing billows
large as smoke.
For instance:
do you wish to be free?

It is too difficult:
you, hooking the distance
catching me   between my thighs;
me, lassoing this space
between our hips
pulling
tight   as a noose.

LETTER, UNSENT

How to tell you
our blood doesn't take us
to the same places...
It is something like that.
The petals of all roses
wither —
you know that old sad story.

The lines
fall off the edge of
the world   as I write
fearing a hundred mid-night
monsters
lying in wait for the lonely.
The gargoyles that greet you
every morning
can't be shared.
The gorgon's eye reflected
in my mirror
pierces me.

In this boat I don't know
where I'm going...
I only know our rivers
separated
somewhere upstream.

WITHIN US THINGS GROW,

the unwanted rising
swelling and filling
more space
than we have
tumors of clay
or abstraction

In these cages
an unholy business
goes on.

AFTER YOU LEAVE, I RISE

to paddle through thick water
The heart beats sweet sweat through all the pores
desire driven from the cells
My thoughts idle about your face
the smell of you, the way you taste

I begin
        to be knotted

with wants.

Wings of white egret
spreading   across a blue sky
close down the camera's shutter
whisper away all the bad dreams, needs
beating at the trap doors
the coiled snake waiting
the clenched fist hammering on these bars
Lift me from the rippling shark's fin
cutting through the water   his mouth ready

to slash
        to swallow

to salt old wounds.

Ah feathered rescuer   you soar
while I stay mud—bound
surveying this slough
choked by weeds   and apprehension
Grazing some inner ear, my thigh unguarded
I play scaleless and solitary   dark lidded eyes

   soothing
           an arrogant

arrangement.

THE SKIN OF THIS ANIMAL

stretches
over an unheated heart

Oh this desire to contain
embrace   embody

to know and to join
hold and hold on to

BE HELD

wrapped in hot fur
forever.

TICKING

The peach-stained moon
has turned white
waiting for this hot night
to end.

All that has been harvested
is time
cut down close
to the bloated root.

What caffeine-filled artifice
keeps my eyes open
under these rays
calling for
more time
        more time...

LUNAR DELUSION

One moon
solitary in her garden of stars
shining her borrowed light
into the shadowed windows
of Paterson or Saratoga Springs
Iowa or Boulder
Bolinas or New York
Slivers of silver prying
into hospitals and prisons
of all kinds

We lie dream—docked
locked in our single births
wrestling our own terrible mysteries
heading for our separate deaths
And when we lie side by side
we think we are not
alone.

SNAKE TRAIL IN THE DUSTY ROAD

What snake has crossed my path
here under these feathered trees
The winding tan dirt road I walk
shows his dusty track
zig-zagging so distinctly
I recoil
hesitating to step over it.

Staring blood-chilled   filled
with dangerous reptillian images
my eyes search the roadside bushes
for the exotic spiral
my ears ready to hear
some warning rustle.

It takes centuries to shed
the cold bumpy skin
and scaly dread slithering
up my spine
and start to walk   me the alien
uncoiling cautiously
into his dense landscape.

THE VOYEUR IN SEARCH OF A LIFE

                I

It is a fishy way to watch things anyway
Sitting in front of this glass scene
I see the lips of people shaping words
a silent movie filled with images
I cannot touch or hear
And all the angles are untrue
in this refraction

I know the distance is always there
But is that me watching them
or them watching me

I didn't laugh much   sing   or dance
observing the habits of humans
riding the bus   waiting for the elevator
waiting for the curtain to rise
I was there watching you
live your lives   standing
outside of mine.

                II

Today
      the wind blows the hard pears down
                        from the tree
                                before their time
    so many
              that will never ripen
                        lie about the ground
    and though still June
           the yellow locust leaves
                      begin to cover the red bricks

Today
      the fog sits thick on the ridge line
           drafts of wind roll down the canyon
                the walls of the house shudder.

III

Now
    here with my teeth
           in the heart of it
    here with my heart
           in the teeth of it
    worrying it
    straddling it
    feeling the tremor
           in the soul

    I am outside this window
               looking in
    I am inside this window
               looking out

Always
    waiting to be the next leaf
        wrenched loose
             of the autumn branch
    drifting
        down
           to feed the soil
                slowly
                    on any wind.

IV

I am sitting in a roomful of women
and think of you
It all seems so episodic   my life

There are times I want to latch on to you
like some tick   looking for a home
ready to go at your pace
            unpack at your hotels
                        celebrate your holidays.

V

I hang on to a thread
draw it through these woods   look back
not to find my way out
but to see
if there really is
a path.

WHAT HAS BEEN ENGINEERED

I am looking for a new house
and have ordered inspections.
Excavation away from
what once was cemented
damages foundations.
In wet weather this interior
footing may not hold.
An engineer has told me,
his report is in writing:
five pages of typed words.

On the flat black roof
tar and gravel have bubbled;
moisture collected below.
There are stains
on the heavy wood beams
of the ceiling   where rains
of past years
have leaked through.

Where the concrete cracks
in the steep driveway
green pushes and eats
the harsh shell.

In the mail letters
from my attorney —
dissolution agreement
filed with the courts.

All the paths into my past
are guarded   and concrete covers
what would otherwise be eroded
too soft   easily washed away
like the lines of a contract
written with felt pen
ready to blur
at the season's first rain.

WORDS AFTER A LAPSE IN WRITING DURING WHICH I MOVE FROM ONE HOUSE TO ANOTHER

I ask why am i doing this
smelling the resins
O.D.ing on fumes
as i finish a door

Watching water
spill from the sky
i've been riding the rainbow
down

Need to arc earth to sky once more
to write again   to write again
to get the fire inside
out
and warm the skin.

MOVED IN AT LAST,

boxes of books unpacked
I look out the sliding glass across the deck
toward the valley.   All the trees
are greyed out like an unpainted picture.
Unusual rain.
Seeds soak in the wooden bird feeder
at the railing's edge.
A blue and black Steller's jay pecks at them
anyway   feathers clumped damply together.
Fished out of the unseasonable weather by the lure
of food, his dark crest looks waterlogged.
He eats until some movement in the lichened pine leaning
over the small house startles him into hasty flight
then dives into the clammy canyon trailing squawks .

I settle solitary into the orange chair
drinking lemon grass tea
from a cup with the handle cracked
in this weekend's move.

It begins to lighten   trees become visible
the painting fills in
and I see where I have come to after all these months.
From a hole in the green mass of tree—tops
grey smoke rises.
Someone has lit a fire.
And over on the mountain side of this house
fog drifts and sidles intimately between ridges.
The flowers on my new neighbor's catalpa trees
drop wet purple petals.   They stick to the stones.

ANOTHER CALAMITY

The rains brought down my bay tree.
Roots torn from soggy earth
it fell a thunderous rumble
toward my neighbor's roof.
Caught by the small catalpa
it leans its heavy gray—barked weight
against the other's fragile wintry limbs;
the wooden house saved from catastrophe.

The lighter branches hit the tar and gravel
like a rain of pebbles
but no damage.
It was the storm I guess.
Some talk of rotten roots.
Who could know that hidden
in the dark earth
there was a secret
weakening.

Thus it goes, we walk the covered surface
of this spinning ball
illusioned with stability   until
      the unexpected cave—in occurs
bolts loosen   knots slip
the fraying ropes that hold our lives together
give way.

WHAT ARE YOU DOING HERE

in this place   where

ego

needs to be covered
with layers of shell
cradled from shocks
encrusted well

or maybe

the shell needs cracking
peeling away
like the black turban on the beach
until the fortressed conceit

floats

in the air

    ribboning out like fog

        or a kite

           then eventually

              let go of

                let go of

DECISIONS

There are rooms I try not to enter
fearing what is final, the jump
that betrays the past
I stand over—long in every doorway —
those strange bridges —
seeing the swamp I choose to hold
within my bones.

If only it were simple
all that is final
coming full circle
The myths of each beginning carry
their endings cradled like the moon
It is a burden to own
we must also start what we finish.

There is no painless way to travel.

THEY WERE, HE WAS, SHE WAS

They were characters in a common play
They were early to bed and early to rise
They were instant incarnations of non–fat acceptable words
Their toes smelled musty
and their warts glowed in the dark
So they kept the lights on.

They were on time   in time   in their time   this time
They invited everyone to their prime time T.V. beef.

They were a bad example of what to do when it rained.
They were waiting to tear the labels off
and they jarred.

They didn't know how to do it any other way.

Then the fog lifted
                    costumes fell

teeth shone   nails broke

wings sprouted
                    And they parted.

He was sorry
He was unable to sew the buttons on
But he got better.

He climbed mountains, ran rivers, ran marathons
He burned
He carried ashes to Mt. Olympus.

He played his hi–fi loud and lowered his pants cuffs.
He trained hair over his lips and let the roses run wild.
He blew his nose on linen and wiped his floors with newsprint.
He ate garlic and drank perrier water.

He was thirsty.

He learned more about how to live by himself.

He sat in his house under redwood trees

He no longer asked:
                      Where did all the people go?

She was free
She went to bed when she pleased
And with whom.

She bought books and studied
She paid the bills late
She pulled fleas off cats, closed her windows to flies
She killed only invaders.

She placed words on paper.
She partied.

She watched pine branches blur the view of the bay.
She wondered about her lungs.

She cried less.
She cried more.
She fought.
She fought daughters and plumbers, mechanics and mothers
and lawyers and doctors and teachers and lovers.

She wanted fire.   She wanted light.

She grew tired.

She slept with her arms around a pillow
She slept curled into herself.

She grew calm.

LOVE AGAIN

Love, that turtle shell
in which i hide
silent behind my teeth
harmless as butter

Love staining my mouth
like blueberries
filling my head
with sugar

Love, that balm
that daisy opener
careless as tin
soothing me away
from paper and words

That skin teasing
flea
it bites
sucks my will
leaves me peeling
like eucalyptus
down to some core
where, at least for today
nothing else matters.

LANGUAGE OF A SMALL SPACE

A forest of different birds
you can know them by their songs
more than their feathers.

I tell myself:
learn to listen.

But the myth of language
is that we can speak
hear each other's words
and separate
all that smoky noise
from what is being said
stripping the frothy fashions
we carry with us
peeling the crusted skin
to get at the heart.

ODE TO ROMANTIC POETRY

While there are still
bells ringing in my blood
and silvered noises flash
between my cells
while flower buds burst
shackles into flame
to wave their frenzied
greeting at the clouds
my limbs can dance
in unbound meter yet
and belts of hammered links
drop to the ground.
Praise all explosions
into life
and wings that soar
avoid the old assassin fear
the arrow's deft precision
and the clammy floor.

THE AWE—FILLED WOUNDS

This morning everything opens
to allow the piercing knives
to nestle in this half—used heart.

I watch the arcs of hummingbirds
carving the blue sky into moorish slices,
hear the red—throated finch
sing its unrecorded message
from black telephone wires,
stroke the warm satin cat
who yesterday stood at the door
with the stiffening mouse in her jaws.

The sweet chilled papaya for breakfast
tastes like perfume...
though tomorrow I may taste once more
some charcoal loaf
or find my wine turned acid.

How the jasmine scents the air
with a thick velvet vapor that stirs
yearning after varied harems, Persian
treasures, silken tents of scarved limbs
bending into braceleted ballets.

I breathe   for a moment
scarred   with joy.

BIOGRAPHICAL NOTE

Deirdre Sharett was born in New York City, grew up in Paterson, New Jersey, and has lived in the Midwest, Pacific Northwest, and the San Francisco Bay Area. She has studied at Drew University, College of Marin, New College of California, and San Francisco State University.